by Iain Gray

Lang**Syne**
PUBLISHING
WRITING *to* REMEMBER

LangSyne

PUBLISHING

WRITING *to* REMEMBER

79 Main Street, Newtongrange,
Midlothian EH22 4NA
Tel: 0131 344 0414   Fax: 0845 075 6085
E-mail: info@lang-syne.co.uk
www.langsyneshop.co.uk

Design by Dorothy Meikle
Printed by Printwell Ltd
© Lang Syne Publishers Ltd 2016

ISBN 978-1-85217-249-7

Donnelly

MOTTO:
Under this sign we are victorious.

CREST:
Two arms bent and counter-crossed,
each holding a sword and with one
transfixing a boar's head and the other a heart
(and) A naked arm rising out of ducal
coronet grasping a dart.

NAME variations include:
ÓDomhnaill *(Gaelic)*
Ó Donnaghaile *(Gaelic)*
Donelly
Donneely
O' Donnell
O' Donnelly

Chapter one:
Origins of Irish surnames

According to an old saying, there are two types of Irish – those who actually are Irish and those who wish they were.

This sentiment is only one example of the allure that the high romance and drama of the proud nation's history holds for thousands of people scattered across the world today.

It's a sad fact, however, that the vast majority of Irish surnames are found far beyond Irish shores, rather than on the Emerald Isle itself.

The population stood at around eight million souls in 1841, but today it stands at fewer than six million.

This is mainly a tragic consequence of the potato famine, also known as the Great Hunger, which devastated Ireland between 1845 and 1849.

The Irish peasantry had become almost wholly reliant for basic sustenance on the potato, first introduced from the Americas in the seventeenth century.

When the crop was hit by a blight, at least 800,000 people starved to death while an estimated two million others were forced to seek a new life far from their native shores – particularly in America, Canada, and Australia.

The effects of the potato blight continued until about 1851, by which time a firm pattern of emigration had become established.

Ireland's loss, however, was to the gain of the countries in which the immigrants settled, contributing enormously, as their descendants do today, to the well being of the nations in which their forefathers settled.

But those who were forced through dire circumstance to establish a new life in foreign parts never forgot their roots, or the proud heritage and traditions of the land that gave them birth.

Nor do their descendants.

It is a heritage that is inextricably bound up in the colourful variety of Irish names themselves – and the origin and history of these names forms an integral part of the vibrant drama that is the nation's history, one of both glorious fortune and tragic misfortune.

This history is well documented, and one of the most important and fascinating of the earliest sources are *The Annals of the Four Masters*, compiled between 1632 and 1636 by four friars at the Franciscan Monastery in County Donegal.

Compiled from earlier sources, and purporting to go back to the Biblical Deluge, much of the material takes in the mythological origins and history of Ireland and the Irish.

This includes tales of successive waves of invaders and settlers such as the Fomorians, the Partholonians, the Nemedians, the Fir Bolgs, the Tuatha De Danann, and the Laigain.

Of particular interest are the *Milesian Genealogies*,

because the majority of Irish clans today claim a descent from either Heremon, Ir, or Heber – three of the sons of Milesius, a king of what is now modern day Spain.

These sons invaded Ireland in the second millennium B.C, apparently in fulfilment of a mysterious prophecy received by their father.

This Milesian lineage is said to have ruled Ireland for nearly 3,000 years, until the island came under the sway of England's King Henry II in 1171 following what is known as the Cambro-Norman invasion.

This is an important date not only in Irish history in general, but for the effect the invasion subsequently had for Irish surnames.

'Cambro' comes from the Welsh, and 'Cambro-Norman' describes those Welsh knights of Norman origin who invaded Ireland.

But they were invaders who stayed, inter-marrying with the native Irish population and founding their own proud dynasties that bore Cambro-Norman names such as Archer, Barbour, Brannagh, Fitzgerald, Fitzgibbon, Fleming, Joyce, Plunkett, and Walsh – to name only a few.

These 'Cambro-Norman' surnames that still flourish throughout the world today form one of the three main categories in which Irish names can be placed – those of Gaelic-Irish, Cambro-Norman, and Anglo-Irish.

Previous to the Cambro-Norman invasion of the twelfth century, and throughout the earlier invasions and settlement of those wild bands of sea rovers known as the Vikings in the eighth and ninth centuries, the population of the island was relatively small, and it was normal for a person to be identified through the use of only a forename.

But as population gradually increased and there were many more people with the same forename, surnames were adopted to distinguish one person, or one community, from another.

Individuals identified themselves with their own particular tribe, or 'tuath', and this tribe – that also became known as a clann, or clan – took its name from some distinguished ancestor who had founded the clan.

The Gaelic-Irish form of the name Kelly, for example, is Ó Ceallaigh, or O'Kelly, indicating descent from an original 'Ceallaigh', with the 'O' denoting 'grandson of.' The name was later anglicised to Kelly.

The prefix 'Mac' or 'Mc', meanwhile, as with the clans of the Scottish Highlands, denotes 'son of.'

Although the Irish clans had much in common with their Scottish counterparts, one important difference lies in what are known as 'septs', or branches, of the clan.

Septs of Scottish clans were groups who often bore an entirely different name from the clan name but were under the clan's protection.

In Ireland, septs were groups that shared the same name and who could be found scattered throughout the four provinces of Ulster, Leinster, Munster, and Connacht.

The 'golden age' of the Gaelic-Irish clans, infused as their veins were with the blood of Celts, pre-dates the Viking invasions of the eighth and ninth centuries and the Norman invasion of the twelfth century, and the sacred heart of the country was the Hill of Tara, near the River Boyne, in County Meath.

Known in Gaelic as 'Teamhar na Rí', or Hill of Kings, it was the royal seat of the 'Ard Rí Éireann', or High King of Ireland, to whom the petty kings, or chieftains, from the island's provinces were ultimately subordinate.

It was on the Hill of Tara, beside a stone pillar known as the Irish 'Lia Fáil', or Stone of Destiny, that the High Kings were inaugurated and, according to legend, this stone would emit a piercing screech that could be heard all over Ireland when touched by the hand of the rightful king.

The Hill of Tara is today one of the island's main tourist attractions.

Opposition to English rule over Ireland, established in the wake of the Cambro-Norman invasion, broke out frequently and the harsh solution adopted by the powerful forces of the Crown was to forcibly evict the native Irish from their lands.

These lands were then granted to Protestant colonists, or 'planters', from Britain.

Many of these colonists, ironically, came from Scotland and were the descendants of the original 'Scotti', or 'Scots', who gave their name to Scotland after migrating there in the fifth century A.D., from the north of Ireland.

Colonisation entailed harsh penal laws being imposed on the majority of the native Irish population, stripping them practically of all of their rights.

The Crown's main bastion in Ireland was Dublin and its environs, known as the Pale, and it was the dispossessed peasantry who lived outside this Pale, desperately striving to eke out a meagre living.

It was this that gave rise to the modern-day expression of someone or something being 'beyond the pale'.

Attempts were made to stamp out all aspects of the ancient Gaelic-Irish culture, to the extent that even to bear a Gaelic-Irish name was to invite discrimination.

This is why many Gaelic-Irish names were anglicised with, for example, and noted above, Ó Ceallaigh, or O'Kelly, being anglicised to Kelly.

Succeeding centuries have seen strong revivals of Gaelic-Irish consciousness, however, and this has led to many families reverting back to the original form of their name, while the language itself is frequently found on the fluent tongues of an estimated 90,000 to 145,000 of the island's population.

Ireland's turbulent history of religious and political strife is one that lasted well into the twentieth century, a landmark century that saw the partition of the island into the twenty-six counties of the independent Republic of

Ireland, or Eire, and the six counties of Northern Ireland, or Ulster.

Dublin, originally founded by Vikings, is now a vibrant and truly cosmopolitan city while the proud city of Belfast is one of the jewels in the crown of Ulster.

It was Saint Patrick who first brought the light of Christianity to Ireland in the fifth century A.D.

Interpretations of this Christian message have varied over the centuries, often leading to bitter sectarian conflict – but the many intricately sculpted Celtic Crosses found all over the island are symbolic of a unity that crosses the sectarian divide.

It is an image that fuses the 'old gods' of the Celts with Christianity.

All the signs from the early years of this new millennium indicate that sectarian strife may soon become a thing of the past – with the Irish and their many kinsfolk across the world, be they Protestant or Catholic, finding common purpose in the rich tapestry of their shared heritage.

Chapter two:
World mighty

**The history of the Donnellys, in all the rich variety of
spellings of the name, is one shot through with myth and
legend, high romance and drama, and both glorious
fortune and tragic misfortune.**

Their roots are to be found in the soil of the present day
county of Donegal, while the name itself indicates a truly
illustrious royal pedigree.

In its Gaelic form of 'O Domhnaill' the name indicates
'world mighty' – a fitting description when we learn that a
founder of the clan was Conall Gulban, a son of the
celebrated Niall Noíghiallach, better known to posterity as
the great warrior king Niall of the Nine Hostages.

The dramatic life and times of this ancestor of the
Donnellys are steeped in stirring Celtic myth and legend.

The youngest son of Eochaidh Mugmedon, king of the
province of Connacht, his mother died in childbirth and he was
brought up by his evil stepmother Mongfhinn who, for reasons
best known to herself, was determined that he should die.

She accordingly abandoned him naked on the Hill of
Tara, inauguration site of the Ard Rí, or High Kings, of
Ireland, but he was found by a wandering bard who took
him back to his father.

One legend is that Mongfhinn sent Niall and his four

brothers – Brian, Fiachra, Ailill, and Fergus – to a renowned prophet who was also a blacksmith to determine which of them would succeed their father as Ard Rí.

The blacksmith, known as Sitchin, set the lads a task by deliberately setting fire to his forge.

Niall's brothers ran in and came out carrying the spearheads, fuel, hammers, and barrels of beer that they had rescued, but Niall staggered out clutching the heavy anvil so vital to the blacksmith's trade.

By this deed, Sitchin prophesied that Niall would be the one who would take on the glorious mantle of kingship.

Another prophetic incident occurred one day while Niall and his brothers were engaged in the hunt.

Thirsty from their efforts they encountered an ugly old woman who offered them water – but only in return for a kiss.

Three of the lads, no doubt repelled by her green teeth and scaly skin, refused. Fiachra pecked her lightly on the cheek and, by this act, she prophesied that he would one day reign at Tara – but only briefly.

The bold Niall, however, kissed her fully on the lips. The hag then demanded that he should now have full sexual intercourse with her and, undaunted, he did so.

Through this action she was suddenly transformed into a stunningly beautiful young woman known as Flaithius, or Royalty, who predicted that he would become the greatest High King of Ireland.

His stepmother Mongfhinn later tried to poison him,

but accidentally took the deadly potion herself and died.

This legend relates to what was known as the Festival of Mongfhinn, or Feis na Samhan (the Fest of Samhain), because it was on the evening of October 31, on Samhain's Eve, that the poisoning incident is said to have taken place.

It was believed for centuries in Ireland that, on Samhain Eve, Mongfhinn's warped and wicked spirit would roam the land in hungry search of children's souls. The Festival, or Feast, of Samhain, is today better known as Halloween.

Niall became Ard Rí in 379 A.D. and embarked on the series of military campaigns and other daring adventures that would subsequently earn him the title of Niall of the Nine Hostages.

The nine countries and territories into which he raided and took hostages for ransom were the Irish provinces of Munster, Leinster, Connacht, and Ulster, Britain, and the territories of the Saxons, Morini, Picts, and Dalriads.

Niall's most famous hostage was a young lad known as Succat, son of Calpernius, a Romano-Briton who lived in the area of present day Milford Haven, on the Welsh coast.

Later known as Patricius, or Patrick, he became renowned as Ireland's patron saint, St. Patrick, responsible for bringing the light of Christianity to the island in the early years of the fifth century A.D.

Raiding in Gaul, in the area of Boulogne-sur-mer in present day France, Niall was ambushed and killed by one of his treacherous subjects in 405 A.D.

While septs of Donnellys were to be found throughout the Emerald Isle, it was the Donnellys descended from Niall's son Conall who would come to dominate the pages of Irish history.

They flourished for centuries as the O' Donnells of Tirconnell – with 'connell' indicating 'Connell' or 'Conall's' territory.

Tirconnell later became known as Donegal, and it was in the area of present day Letterkenny that the Donnelly chieftains were solemnly inaugurated.

Niall's sons founded what became the mighty tribal groupings of the northern Uí Neill and the southern Uí Neill, and it was as part of the northern Uí Neill that the Ulster Donnellys held the honoured and important hereditary position of marshals of the forces of the powerful northern O' Neills.

The fortunes of both proud clans became inextricably linked as they fought off successive waves of invaders and struggled to defend their ancient rights and privileges.

What would subsequently prove to be the event that sowed the seeds of the destruction of the Gaelic way of life of proud native Irish clans such as the Donnellys and the O' Neills came in the late twelfth century – with the Cambro-Norman invasion and the subsequent consolidation of the power of the English Crown over the island.

Twelfth century Ireland was far from being a unified nation, split up as it was into territories ruled over by squabbling chieftains who ruled as kings in their own right – and this inter-clan rivalry worked to the advantage of the invaders.

In a series of bloody conflicts one chieftain, or king, would occasionally gain the upper hand over his rivals, and by 1156 the strongest was Muirchertach MacLochlainn, king of the powerful O'Neills.

He was opposed by the equally powerful Rory O'Connor, king of the province of Connacht, but he increased his power and influence by allying himself with Dermot MacMurrough, king of Leinster.

MacLochlainn and MacMurrough were aware that the main key to the kingdom of Ireland was the thriving trading port of Dublin that had been established by invading Vikings, or Ostmen, in 852 A.D.

Dublin was taken by the combined forces of the Leinster and Connacht kings, but when MacLochlainn died the Dubliners rose up in revolt and overthrew the unpopular MacMurrough. A triumphant Rory O'Connor entered Dublin and was later inaugurated as Ard Rí, but MacMurrough refused to accept defeat.

He appealed for help from England's King Henry II in unseating O'Connor – an act that was to radically affect the future course of Ireland's fortunes in general and those of the Donnellys and other native Irish clans in particular.

The English king agreed to help MacMurrough, but distanced himself from direct action by delegating his Norman subjects in Wales with the task.

These ambitious and battle-hardened barons and knights had first settled in Wales following the Norman Conquest of England in 1066 and, with an eye on rich booty, plunder, and lands, were only too eager to obey their sovereign's wishes and furnish MacMurrough with aid.

MacMurrough rallied powerful barons such as Robert Fitzstephen and Maurice Fitzgerald to his cause, along with Gilbert de Clare, Earl of Pembroke.

The mighty Norman war machine soon moved into action, and so fierce and disciplined was their onslaught on the forces of Rory O'Connor and his allies that by 1171 they had re-captured Dublin and other strategically important territories.

Henry II now began to take cold feet over the venture, realising that he may have created a rival in the form of a separate Norman kingdom in Ireland.

Accordingly, he landed on the island, near Waterford, at the head of a large army in October of 1171 with the aim of curbing the power of his Cambro-Norman barons.

But protracted war between the king and his barons was averted when they submitted to the royal will, promising homage and allegiance in return for holding the territories they had conquered in the king's name.

Henry also received the submission and homage of many of the Irish chieftains – but the Ulster clans such as the Donnellys and the O'Neills were resolute in their defiance.

Chapter three:

Swords of rebellion

English dominion over Ireland was ratified through the Treaty of Windsor of 1175, but it only served to sow the seeds of a series of rebellions that would set the island ablaze over succeeding centuries.

An indication of the harsh treatment meted out to the native Irish can be found in a desperate plea sent to Pope John XII by Roderick O'Carroll of Ely, Donald O'Neill of Ulster, and a number of other Irish chieftains in 1318.

They stated: 'As it very constantly happens, whenever an Englishman, by perfidy or craft, kills an Irishman, however noble, or however innocent, be he clergy or layman, there is no penalty or correction enforced against the person who may be guilty of such wicked murder.

'But rather the more eminent the person killed and the higher rank which he holds among his own people, so much more is the murderer honoured and rewarded by the English, and not merely by the people at large, but also by the religious and bishops of the English race.'

There were actually three separate Irelands.

These were the territories of the privileged and powerful Norman barons and their retainers, the Ireland of the disaffected Gaelic-Irish such as the Donnellys who held lands unoccupied by the Normans, and the Pale – comprised of Dublin itself and a substantial area of its environs ruled over by an English elite.

In common with their clan counterparts in the Highlands and Islands of Scotland the native Irish clans, when not engaged in warfare with the English, became embroiled in often bitter and bloody disputes with one another.

This was no less the case than with the Donnellys.

The mid-sixteenth century Donnelly chieftain, Manus, was imprisoned by his son, Calvagh, after he had submitted to the English Crown.

With the benefit of historical hindsight, Manus had been left with little option but to do so.

His rebellion had followed a bold but ultimately futile attempt by he and the O'Neills to attack the Pale and oust the ruling English elite installed in Dublin.

Complex and internecine warfare among the Donnellys themselves followed until Hugh Dubh O'Donnell was eventually inaugurated as Chieftain.

While these quarrels do not mark a particularly edifying period in their otherwise proud history, honour was restored on the national stage through Hugh Dubh's son Aodh Rua Ó Domhmaill, better known to posterity as Red Hugh O'Donnell, and who was born in 1571.

Taking on the mantle of the Donnelly chieftainship at the age of 26, Red Hugh had experienced hardship from the age of 17 when he and the brothers Art and Henry O'Neill, were kidnapped on the orders of the English Lord Deputy in Ireland, Sir John Perrot, and imprisoned in Dublin Castle.

It was in the gripping cold of the winter of 1582 that they managed to escape, aided along the way by a number of sympathetic native Irish clans that included the O' Byrnes and the O' Tooles.

But by the time the safety of the O' Donnell stronghold of the castle of Ballyshannon, in Donegal, was reached Art O' Neill had died from exposure and Red Hugh had lost his two big toes to frostbite.

In the meantime discontent had grown over the policy known as 'plantation', or settlement of loyal Protestants on lands previously held by the native Irish.

This policy had started during the reign from 1491 to 1547 of Henry VIII, whose Reformation effectively outlawed the established Roman Catholic faith throughout his dominions.

This plantation continued throughout the subsequent reigns of Elizabeth I, James I (James VI of Scotland), Charles I, and in the aftermath of the Cromwellian invasion of the island in 1649.

Rebellion erupted in 1594 against the increasingly harsh treatment of the native Irish and its forefront was Red Hugh.

In what became known as the Cogadh na Naoi mBliama, or the Nine Years War, Red Hugh and his skilled Donnelly and other kinsfolk, such as the Gallaghers, literally set the island ablaze in a vicious campaign of guerrilla warfare.

It was under the inspired leadership of Red Hugh that a whirlwind of devastation was inflicted on English settlements and garrisons in a daring series of lightning raids.

In 1596, allied with the forces of Hugh O'Neill, Earl of Tyrone, Red Hugh inflicted a defeat on an English army at the battle of Clontibert, while in August of 1598 another significant defeat was inflicted at the battle of Yellow Ford.

As English control over Ireland teetered on the brink of collapse, thousands of more troops, including mercenaries, were hastily despatched to the island and, in the face of the overwhelming odds against them, Red Hugh and the Earl of Tyrone sought help from England's enemy, Spain.

A well-equipped Spanish army under General del Aquila landed at Kinsale in December of 1601, but was forced into surrender only a few weeks later, in January of 1602.

Resistance continued until 1603, but proved abortive.

As the Donnellys sought refuge where they could, Red Hugh O'Donnell had already been forced to flee to Spain, where he died in 1602.

Five years later, in September of 1607 and in what is known as The Flight of the Earls, Rory O' Donnell, Red Hugh's brother, and Hugh O'Neill, 2nd Earl of Tyrone, sailed into foreign exile from the village of Rathmullan, on the shores of Lough Swilly, in the Donnelly homeland of Co. Donegal, accompanied by ninety loyal followers.

This, in the opinion of many scholars, represented the collapse of the old Gaelic order.

The final collapse came through what is known in Ireland as Cogadh an Dá Rí, or The War of the Two Kings.

Also known as the Williamite War in Ireland or the Jacobite War in Ireland, it was sparked off in 1688 when the Stuart monarch James II (James VII of Scotland) was deposed and fled into exile in France.

The Protestant William of Orange and his wife Mary (ironically a daughter of James II) were invited to take up the thrones of Scotland, Ireland, and England – but James still had significant support in Ireland.

His supporters were known as Jacobites, and among them were several Donnellys.

Following the arrival in England of William and Mary from Holland, Richard Talbot, 1st Earl of Tyrconnell and James's Lord Deputy in Ireland, assembled an army loyal to the Stuart cause.

The aim was to garrison and fortify the island in the name of James and quell any resistance.

Londonderry, or Derry, proved loyal to the cause of William of Orange, or William III as he had become, and managed to hold out against a siege that was not lifted until July 28, 1689.

James, with the support of troops and money supplied by Louis XIV of France, had landed at Kinsale in March of 1689 and joined forces with his Irish supporters.

A series of military encounters followed, culminating in

James's defeat by an army commanded by William at the battle of the Boyne on July 12, 1689.

The Williamite forces besieged Limerick and the Jacobites were forced into surrender in September of 1691.

A peace treaty, known as the Treaty of Limerick followed, under which those Jacobites willing to swear an oath of loyalty to William were allowed to remain in their native land.

Those reluctant to do so included many native Irish such as the Donnellys.

Among them was Daniel O' Donnell, who carried in his battered luggage to France a precious Donnelly relic known as the Cathach.

Compiled by no less a figure than St. Colmcille, better known in Scotland as St. Columba and, along with St. Patrick and St. Bridget one of the three patron saints of Ireland, it was a book of psalms known as the 'battle book' of the ancient Donnelly warriors.

The sixth century saint was a close kinsman of the Donnellys, on whose behalf he compiled the book that would be carried into battle at the head of their warriors.

The book lay for several centuries in a monastery after being taken to France by Daniel O' Donnell and, after being spotted by chance by a priest in the late nineteenth century, eventually found its way back to its native land.

This enduring legacy of the Donnellys, encased in a magnificent silver shrine, is now one of the treasures of the National Museum in Dublin.

Chapter four:

On the world stage

Donnellys, in the all the rich variety of spellings of the name, have achieved international fame and distinction in a range of pursuits.

Born in 1947 in Teaneck, New Jersey, **Jamie Donnelly** is the American actress and acting coach best known for her role as Jan in the film version of the musical *Grease* that also starred Olivia Newton John and John Travolta.

Across the ocean to the United Kingdom **Declan Donnelly**, better known as 'Dec', is the British entertainer born in 1975 in Newcastle upon Tyne.

Along with his partner Anthony 'Ant' McPartlin he is one half of the 'Ant and Dec' television presenting team.

At the time of writing he and his partner are probably best known for presenting the popular British television series *I'm A Celebrity … Get Me Out of Here!*

Born in 1931 in Bradford, England, but raised in Dublin, **Donal Donnelly** is the talented theatre and movie actor now resident in the United States, while in the world of the printed word the grandly named **Ignatius Loyola Donnelly** was the writer best known for his work on the mythical lost continent of Atlantis.

Born in 1831 in Philadelphia, he also served for a time

as lieutenant governor of Minnesota and as Republican Congressman for Minnesota.

His best-known literary work was *Atlantis: The Antediluvian World*, published nearly twenty years before his death in 1901, and still a best seller today.

In the original Donnelly homeland of Ireland **Peader O' Donnell**, born in 1893 in Donegal and who died in 1986, was the political activist and writer whose best-known work remains the novel *Islanders*.

He also for a time edited the Irish literary magazine *The Bell*.

Another Irish political activist and writer was **Charles Donnelly**, born in 1914 in Killybrackey, Co. Tyrone, and who died in 1937.

Involved in both the Irish Republican movement and the Communist Party of Ireland, he joined the International Brigades that fought on the Republican side during the Spanish Civil War.

He had been only a few short weeks in Spain when, in February of 1937, he was killed in action. Shortly before his death, during a brief lull in the fighting, he had picked up a bunch of olives and uttered what has now become the famous line of 'Even the olives are bleeding.'

A collection of his poems was published in 1987.

Also on the field of battle **Major Michael Donnelly**, born in 1959, became a prominent activist for sufferers of

Gulf War Syndrome after serving with the United States Air Force during the first Gulf War.

The author of *Falcon's Cry: A Desert Storm Memoir*, he died in 2005.

From the battlefield to the highly competitive world of sport **Sharon Donnelly**, born in 1967 in Toronto, is the Canadian athlete who took the gold medal for the gruelling triathlon event at the 1999 Pan American games in Winnipeg.

She is now a triathlon coach.

In the world of Major League Baseball **Brendan Donnolly**, born in 1971 in Washington D.C., is the talented pitcher who, at the time of writing, plays with the Boston Red Sox.

On the football pitch **Simon Donnelly**, born in 1974 in Glasgow, is the Scottish midfielder who, at the time of writing, has been capped ten times for his country and plays for Partick Thistle.

He has also played for teams that include Celtic, Sheffield Wednesday, St. Johnstone, and Dunfermline Athletic.

Born in 1953 in Glasgow **Dougie Donnelly** is a popular British television sports broadcaster who began his career in Scottish radio, while on the tennis court **Gary Donnelly**, born in 1962 in Phoenix, Arizona, is a former American professional player.

In the world of ecclesiastical affairs **James O' Donnell**, born in 1738 in Tipperary, was the Franciscan friar who became known as the 'Apostle of Newfoundland.'

He was Prior to the Franciscan House in the Irish east coast port of Waterford at a time when there was a great deal of contact by sea between the port and Newfoundland.

A number of Newfoundland merchants asked for him to be sent to Newfoundland – and it was there that he arrived in 1796, contributing greatly to the religious and political life of his new homeland until his death in 1811.

Born in 1856 in Kilraine, Co. Donegal, **Patrick O' Donnell** became, at the age of 24, the youngest bishop in the world at the time.

By 1914 he was a cardinal and, up until his death in 1927, was involved in not only an impressive range of church and school building projects but also in campaigns for the restoration of the ancient Gaelic-Irish language.

He was also a founder member of the National University of Ireland.

In the world of contemporary music **Tanya Donelly**, born in 1966 in Newport, Rhode Island, is the Grammy-nominated singer, songwriter, and guitarist who achieved fame as the lead singer and songwriter for the band Belly.

Along with her stepsister Kristin Hersh she is co-founder of the band Throwing Muses.

Donnellys have been, and continue to be, prominent in the often cut-throat world of politics.

Born in 1891 in Lebanon, Missouri, **Phil M. Donnelly**

served as Democrat Governor of Missouri from between 1945 to 1949 and from between 1953 to 1957, while **Brian Donnelly**, born in 1949, is the New Zealand politician who is a member of the New Zealand First Party.

Born in 1946 in Dorchester, Boston, **Brian J. Donnelly** served as the Democrat Representative for Massachusetts from 1979 until 1993, and later as U.S. Ambassador to Trinidad and Tobago.

In Canada, **Fin Donnelly** is the politician and environmental activist whose passion is raising awareness of the rivers and watersheds of British Columbia.

Accordingly, he has made at least fourteen swims of British Columbia's lakes and rivers in addition to serving as executive director of the Rivershed Society of British Columbia.

Still in Canada **The Black Donnellys** was the name given to a notorious family who immigrated from Co. Tipperary to the village of Lucan, in the township of Biddulph, Middlesex County, Ontario, in about 1845.

The family included James Donnelly, his wife Johannah, seven sons, and a male cousin and young neice who later joined them from Ireland.

They immediately became embroiled in a bitter dispute that had been in existence in the township for some time among Irish immigrants and other settlers.

Sabotage and murder were the order of the day as rival families battled with one another, but the feud reached a gruesomely murderous conclusion in February of 1880 when a vigilante group of about 30 townsfolk known, rather ironically, as the Biddulph Peace Society, attacked the Donnelly homestead.

Five of the family were brutally beaten to death while one of the sons was later shot.

The perpetrators were brought to trial, only for it to end in a hung jury, while a further trial was held but later abandoned because of fears over further murderous civic unrest.

The tale of the Black Donnellys remains a matter of heated controversy in Biddulph Township to this very day.

Key dates in Ireland's history from the first settlers to the formation of the Irish Republic:

circa 7000 B.C.	Arrival and settlement of Stone Age people.
circa 3000 B.C.	Arrival of settlers of New Stone Age period.
circa 600 B.C.	First arrival of the Celts.
200 A.D.	Establishment of Hill of Tara, Co. Meath, as seat of the High Kings.
circa 432 A.D.	Christian mission of St. Patrick.
800-920 A.D.	Invasion and subsequent settlement of Vikings.
1002 A.D.	Brian Boru recognised as High King.
1014	Brian Boru killed at battle of Clontarf.
1169-1170	Cambro-Norman invasion of the island.
1171	Henry II claims Ireland for the English Crown.
1366	Statutes of Kilkenny ban marriage between native Irish and English.
1529-1536	England's Henry VIII embarks on religious Reformation.
1536	Earl of Kildare rebels against the Crown.
1541	Henry VIII declared King of Ireland.
1558	Accession to English throne of Elizabeth I.
1565	Battle of Affane.
1569-1573	First Desmond Rebellion.
1579-1583	Second Desmond Rebellion.
1594-1603	Nine Years War.
1606	Plantation' of Scottish and English settlers.

1607	Flight of the Earls.
1632-1636	Annals of the Four Masters compiled.
1641	Rebellion over policy of plantation and other grievances.
1649	Beginning of Cromwellian conquest.
1688	Flight into exile in France of Catholic Stuart monarch James II as Protestant Prince William of Orange invited to take throne of England along with his wife, Mary.
1689	William and Mary enthroned as joint monarchs; siege of Derry.
1690	Jacobite forces of James defeated by William at battle of the Boyne (July) and Dublin taken.
1691	Athlone taken by William; Jacobite defeats follow at Aughrim, Galway, and Limerick; conflict ends with Treaty of Limerick (October) and Irish officers allowed to leave for France.
1695	Penal laws introduced to restrict rights of Catholics; banishment of Catholic clergy.
1704	Laws introduced constricting rights of Catholics in landholding and public office.
1728	Franchise removed from Catholics.
1791	Foundation of United Irishmen republican movement.
1796	French invasion force lands in Bantry Bay.
1798	Defeat of Rising in Wexford and death of United Irishmen leaders Wolfe Tone and Lord Edward Fitzgerald.

1800	Act of Union between England and Ireland.
1803	Dublin Rising under Robert Emmet.
1829	Catholics allowed to sit in Parliament.
1845-1849	The Great Hunger: thousands starve to death as potato crop fails and thousands more emigrate.
1856	Phoenix Society founded.
1858	Irish Republican Brotherhood established.
1873	Foundation of Home Rule League.
1893	Foundation of Gaelic League.
1904	Foundation of Irish Reform Association.
1913	Dublin strikes and lockout.
1916	Easter Rising in Dublin and proclamation of an Irish Republic.
1917	Irish Parliament formed after Sinn Fein election victory.
1919-1921	War between Irish Republican Army and British Army.
1922	Irish Free State founded, while six northern counties remain part of United Kingdom as Northern Ireland, or Ulster; civil war up until 1923 between rival republican groups.
1949	Foundation of Irish Republic after all remaining constitutional links with Britain are severed.